# HOW TO BE THE BEST GRANDMA IN THE WORLD

A.J. Lowrie

Copyright © 2023 A.J. Lowrie

All rights reserved

The information contained in this book is intended for educational and informational purposes only. The author and publisher do not accept any liability for actions arising from the content of this book or for any errors or omissions. Readers are encouraged to seek professional advice before engaging in any activities or making any decisions based on the information contained in this book.

The views expressed in this book are those of the author and do not necessarily reflect the views of the publisher. The author and publisher make no representation or warranties of any kind with regard to the accuracy, completeness, or suitability of the information contained in this book for any purpose.

No part of this book may be reproduced, or stored in a retrieval system, or transmitted in any form or by any means, electronic, mechanical, photocopying, recording, or otherwise, without express written permission of the publisher.

ISBN-13: 9798394558108

Cover design by: A.J. Lowrie
Images created by: A.J. Lowrie

# CONTENTS

Title Page
Copyright
CHAPTER 1 - Introduction to Grandparenting — 1
CHAPTER 2 - Understanding Your Grandchild — 6
CHAPTER 3 - Building Strong Relationships with your Adult Children — 11
CHAPTER 4 - Creating a Safe Environment for Your Grandchildren — 15
CHAPTER 5 - Nurturing Your Grandchildren's Growth and Development — 19
CHAPTER 6 - Encouraging Creativity Through Playtime — 24
CHAPTER 7 - Supporting Your Grandchildren's Emotional Well-being — 28
CHAPTER 8 - Making Memories with your Family — 32
CHAPTER 9 - Financial Planning for your Grandchildren — 36
CHAPTER 10 - Passing on Cultural Heritage to Future Generations — 40
CHAPTER 11 - Maintaining a Healthy Lifestyle — 44
CHAPTER 12 - The Importance of Grandparenting in Single-Parent Households — 48
CHAPTER 13 - Accepting Changes as Your Grandchildren Grow — 52

| | |
|---|---|
| CHAPTER 14 - Being an Advocate for your Grandchildren's Education | 56 |
| CHAPTER 15 - Encouraging Socialization Skills in your Grandkids | 60 |
| CHAPTER 16 - Managing Behavioural Issues Effectively | 64 |
| CHAPTER 17 - Bonding With Teenage Grandchildren | 68 |
| CHAPTER 18 - Approaching Sensitive Topics with Your Grandchildren | 71 |
| CHAPTER 19 - Surviving Long-distance Relationships with your grandkids | 75 |
| CHAPTER 20 - Leaving A Legacy As The Best Grandma In The World | 79 |
| About The Author | 85 |

# CHAPTER 1 - INTRODUCTION TO GRANDPARENTING

As a grandmother, there is perhaps no greater joy than watching your grandchildren grow up and thrive. But being a great grandma is not just about spoiling them with gifts and treats. It's about being an integral part of their lives, providing guidance, support, and unconditional love.

In this book, I want to share with you my insights on how to be the best grandma in the world. Drawing from my own experiences as a grandmother of five wonderful grandkids, as well as advice from other grandmothers, I'll share practical tips and strategies on everything from building strong relationships with your grandkids to managing conflicts with their parents.

Throughout the book, I'll also delve into some of the most important aspects of being a great grandma – including how to create meaningful memories together, how to encourage your grandkids to pursue their passions and dreams, and how to be there for them during tough times.

Whether you're a new grandma or have been one for years, this book will provide you with plenty of inspiration and practical advice on how to truly make a difference in the lives of your grandchildren. So let's dive in – it's time to become the best grandma in the world!

## Introduction to Grandparenting

Welcome to the wonderful world of grandparenting! Whether you are a first-time grandparent or an experienced one, being a grandparent is one of life's greatest joys. In this chapter, we will explore the importance of grandparenting, the role of a grandparent in a child's life, the changes in modern grandparenting styles, and the challenges and rewards that come with being a grandparent.

## Importance of Grandparenting

Grandparents are an essential part of a child's life. They provide love, guidance, and support that is unique from that given by parents. Research has shown that grandparents have a positive impact on their grandchildren's well-being by promoting emotional stability and reducing stress levels. Children who have strong relationships with their grandparents tend to be more resilient and confident in their personal lives.

In addition to benefiting grandchildren directly, grandparents also benefit from these relationships. Being involved in your grandchildren's lives can help you feel more purposeful and fulfilled as you age. It can also give you a sense of continuity and legacy as you pass down family values and traditions.

## The Role of a Grandparent in a Child's Life

While every grandparent-grandchild relationship is unique, there are some common roles that most grandparents play in their grandchildren's lives:

- ❖ Nurturer: Grandparents often provide comfort, care, and affection for their grandchildren.

- ❖ Teacher: Grandparents share knowledge about family history, culture, values or teach new skills such as arts & crafts or cooking.

- ❖ Mentor: Grandparents offer guidance on big-picture issues like career choices or financial management.
- ❖ Friend: Many grandparents develop close friendships with their grandchildren - playing games together talking sharing stories etc), which can make them feel valued.

**The Changes in Modern Grandparenting Styles**

While the role of grandparenting has remained constant over time - giving unconditional love, support, and guidance - the way grandparents interact with their grandchildren has changed. In modern grandparenting, grandparents are more likely to take an active role in their grandchild's life, rather than just babysitting occasionally.

In some cases, grandparents are even raising their grandchildren full-time, either as legal guardians or because of family circumstances like divorce or a parent's illness. Technology also plays a big role in modern grandparenting. With tools like FaceTime and Skype, grandparents can stay connected with their grandkids more easily from afar.

**Challenges and Rewards**

Like any relationship, being a grandparent can have its challenges. One common challenge is managing expectations between generations. Grandparents may have different ideas about parenting styles or discipline than their adult children do, which can cause tension. It's essential to communicate openly and respectfully about expectations to maintain healthy relationships.

Another challenge arises when distance separates grandparents and grandchildren physically. Making time for visits or video calls can be challenging when schedules don't align.

Despite these challenges, the rewards of grandparenting outweigh them. Watching your grandchildren grow up is one of life's great joys - there is nothing quite like seeing them achieve milestones or accomplish goals they set for themselves.

In conclusion, the importance of grandparenting cannot be overstated: it provides children with love and support while benefiting grandparents in return with purpose and fulfilment as we age. The role of a grandparent varies depending on many factors but nurturing, teaching mentoring & befriending are often common roles that most grandparents play in their grandchildren's lives.

Technology has made staying connected easier than ever before; however, distance still remains one of the biggest challenges faced by modern-day grandparents.

Through it all though the joys & rewards far exceed any challenges that come along the way!

# CHAPTER 2 - UNDERSTANDING YOUR GRANDCHILD

As a grandma, one of the most important things you can do is to understand your grandchild. Every child is unique and special in their own way, and it's important to take the time to get to know them as individuals.

Understanding the different stages of a child's development is key to building a strong relationship with your grandchild. From infancy through adolescence, children go through many changes physically, emotionally, and mentally. Understanding these stages will help you communicate better with your grandchild and tailor your interactions to their specific developmental needs.

Infancy is the first stage of a child's development. During this time, they are completely dependent on their caregivers for all their needs. As a new grandma, it's important to remember that babies need lots of love, attention, and care. Holding them close, feeding them when they're hungry, changing diapers promptly - these are all ways you can bond with your grandchild during this stage.

As your grandchild grows into toddlerhood (around 1-3 years old), they begin to develop more independence and language skills. They may start testing boundaries and expressing their wants and needs more assertively. This can be challenging for some grandparents who are used to being in charge - but it's important to remember that toddlers need safe spaces where they can explore and learn on their own terms.

Pre-schoolers (around 3-5 years old) continue to build on their language skills and cognitive abilities. They start developing friendships outside of the family unit and may have more complex emotions like jealousy or empathy. As a grandma, this is an exciting time because you can start playing games with your grandchild or reading books together.

School-age children (around 6-12 years old) are becoming more independent in all aspects of life - from learning at school to socializing with friends. As a grandma, you may want to make yourself available for homework help or after-school activities like playing sports or doing crafts together.

Adolescence (around 13-18 years old) is a time of significant change for your grandchild. They are navigating the challenges of puberty, relationships, and developing their own sense of identity. During this stage, it's important to respect your grandchild's need for privacy while also being available to offer guidance and support when they need it.

In addition to understanding the different stages of development, it's important to recognize common behavioural patterns in children. For example, tantrums are typical in toddlers as they struggle to communicate their needs effectively. School-age children may become more moody as hormones kick in and they start encountering social pressures outside of the family unit.

By recognizing these patterns, you can respond empathetically and calmly instead of reacting with frustration or anger. Remember - children are still learning how to navigate the world around them, and your role as a grandma is to guide them through these ups and downs.

Effective communication skills are also essential for building a strong relationship with your grandchild. Communication involves not just talking but also listening and understanding each other's perspectives. Here are some tips for communicating effectively:

- ❖ Show interest in what your grandchild has to say: Ask open-ended questions about their day or their interests. Listen actively without interrupting or judging.
- ❖ Use positive reinforcement: Praise your grandchild for their accomplishments, no matter how small. Encourage them when they face challenges by reminding them of past successes.
- ❖ Be honest and straightforward: If you need to have a difficult conversation with your grandchild (such as discussing rules or boundaries), be clear about your

expectations while also respecting their feelings and opinions.

- ❖ Use age-appropriate language: As mentioned earlier, children go through different stages of development that affect their cognitive abilities and language skills. Make sure you adjust your language accordingly so that you're communicating on their level.

- ❖ Model good communication skills: Children learn by watching and imitating. By modelling good communication skills, you can help your grandchild develop these skills themselves.

Finally, bonding with your grandchild is the heart of being the best grandma in the world. Bonding is about creating positive memories and experiences that reinforce your relationship with each other. Here are some ideas for bonding activities:

- ❖ Read books or tell stories together: Sharing stories is a great way to connect emotionally and intellectually with your grandchild.

- ❖ Cook or bake together: Cooking or baking teaches valuable life skills while also providing opportunities for fun and creativity.

- ❖ Play games or do puzzles together: Games and puzzles can be challenging but also rewarding when completed successfully. This teaches perseverance and problem-solving skills.

- ❖ Explore nature together: Spending time outdoors in nature can be an excellent way to bond while also encouraging a love of the natural world.

- ❖ Go on adventures: Whether it's a day trip to a nearby town or a more extended vacation, going on adventures creates special memories that you'll both cherish for years to come.

In conclusion, understanding your grandchild involves recognizing their unique developmental needs, behavioural patterns, and effective communication skills while participating in bonding activities tailored to their interests and abilities. Being the best grandma in the world means taking an active role in their lives by supporting them through challenges, celebrating their accomplishments, and creating positive lifelong memories together.

# CHAPTER 3 - BUILDING STRONG RELATIONSHIPS WITH YOUR ADULT CHILDREN

Congratulations, you've raised your children and they have grown into successful adults. But the job of being a parent is never truly finished. Now that they are adults, it's important to continue building strong relationships with them. In this chapter, we'll discuss how to understand the needs and expectations of your adult children, manage conflicts, and find common ground.

**Understanding the Needs and Expectations of Your Adult Children**

As our children grow up and move out of our homes, their needs and expectations change. It's important to recognize these changes as they impact how we interact with them as parents. Here are some things to keep in mind:

- ❖ Respect their independence – Remember that your adult children are now independent individuals who make their own decisions. As much as you may want to help or offer advice, it's important to respect their independence.

- ❖ Be a good listener – Your adult children may be dealing with new challenges or situations that you haven't experienced before. Listen carefully to what they have to say without judging or offering unsolicited advice.

- ❖ Recognize their achievements – Show your children that you're proud of their accomplishments by acknowledging their successes.

- ❖ Maintain boundaries – Just because your children are adults doesn't mean you have unlimited access to their lives or that they should feel entitled to yours either. Respect each other's boundaries so everyone can feel respected and comfortable.

## Managing Conflicts and Strengthening Relationships

No relationship is perfect, but conflicts can strain even the strongest bonds between family members if not managed properly. How do you handle conflicts while maintaining strong relationships with your adult children? Here are some tips:

- ❖ Communicate openly – Open communication is essential in any relationship, including those between parents and their adult children. If there's an issue or conflict brewing, address it directly rather than avoiding it altogether.

- ❖ Take responsibility for mistakes – We're all human and we make mistakes. If you've done something wrong, take responsibility for it and apologize.

- ❖ Let go of grudges – It's not healthy to hold onto grudges or continue to bring up past conflicts. Learn from past mistakes but focus on moving forward.

- ❖ Don't be afraid to seek outside help – Sometimes conflicts are too difficult to handle alone. Seeking the help of a professional therapist can allow both parties to address their concerns in a neutral environment.

## Finding Common Ground

As we get older, we may find that our interests diverge from those of our adult children. But that doesn't mean there aren't shared passions or activities that can bring us together as a family. Here's how:

- ❖ Make time for shared activities – Create opportunities to do things together that you both enjoy, such as cooking classes or hikes in nature.

- ❖ Celebrate special occasions together – Birthdays, holidays and other special occasions provide great opportunities for family gatherings and creating new memories with your adult children.

- ❖ Foster shared interests – Take an interest in your children's hobbies and passions so you can share experiences with them.

- ❖ Be curious about their lives – Ask questions about what is going on in their lives, without intruding too much into their personal space.

In conclusion, building strong relationships with our adult children takes effort, patience and understanding on both sides. By respecting each other's independence, maintaining open communication, managing conflicts positively and finding common ground through shared activities and mutual interests - you can build the kind of relationship with your adult children that will support them as they navigate life's challenges while also giving you the chance to be the best grandparent possible.

# CHAPTER 4 - CREATING A SAFE ENVIRONMENT FOR YOUR GRANDCHILDREN

As a grandparent, one of your top priorities is ensuring the safety and well-being of your grandchildren. While spending time together can be fun and rewarding, it's important to keep in mind that young children are naturally curious and may not recognize potential dangers around them. Therefore, it's essential to create a safe environment for them to play and explore in.

**Factors that Affect Safety at Home**

There are many factors that can affect the safety of your home when your grandchildren come over to visit. One of the most common concerns is physical hazards such as sharp objects or slippery floors. Other factors include:

- ❖ Age-appropriateness of toys and activities
- ❖ Electrical hazards
- ❖ Chemicals and toxins

- ❖ Medication safety
- ❖ Fire hazards

Identifying these factors is the first step in creating a safe environment for your grandchildren.

**How to Keep Your Home Safe for Kids**

Now that you have identified potential safety risks, it's time to take action and make changes around the house. Here are some tips on how to keep your home safe for kids:

- ❖ Store hazardous items out of reach: Keep sharp objects, cleaning supplies, medications, alcohol and other potentially harmful items locked away or stored up high where little hands cannot reach them.
- ❖ Secure furniture: Heavy furniture such as bookcases or dressers should be anchored securely to the wall using brackets or straps, so they don't fall over if climbed on by a child.
- ❖ Use age-appropriate toys: Make sure toys are appropriate for the age of your grandchild and do not pose any choking hazards.
- ❖ Cover electrical outlets: Use outlet covers or plug protectors to prevent children from sticking their fingers or objects into sockets which could result in electric shock.
- ❖ Keep floors clean and dry: To prevent slips and falls, ensure floors are kept clean and dry. Use rugs with nonslip backing and clean up spills immediately.
- ❖ Install smoke detectors: Make sure there are working smoke detectors in all rooms and that they are tested regularly.
- ❖ Precautions in the kitchen: Store sharp knives and other

utensils out of reach. Keep hot pots and pans on the back burners of the stove and use oven mitts when handling them.

- ❖ Secure windows: Windows should be locked or have window guards installed to prevent children from falling out or getting their fingers caught.

**Emergency Preparedness Measures**

Even with all these precautions, accidents can still happen, so it's important to be prepared for emergencies. As a grandparent, you should have a plan in place for what to do in case of an emergency.

- ❖ Have a first-aid kit: Keep a well-stocked first-aid kit on hand that includes bandages, antiseptic cream, gauze, and other supplies needed for minor injuries.

- ❖ Know CPR: Take a CPR class so you know how to perform basic life-saving techniques if needed.

- ❖ Have emergency contact information: Keep a list of emergency phone numbers including your paediatrician, poison control centre, fire department, police department and hospital near your phone or posted where it is easily accessible.

- ❖ Fire safety: Create an escape plan in case of a fire with designated meeting areas outside the home where everyone can gather safely. Practice this plan regularly with your grandchildren so they know what to do in case of an actual emergency.

- ❖ Be ready for severe weather: Depending on where you live you may need to be prepared for severe weather such as hurricanes or tornadoes by having an emergency kit stocked with food, water, flashlights, and other essential items.

In conclusion, creating a safe environment for your grandchildren is essential when they come over to visit. Evaluate potential hazards around the house and take steps to mitigate risks by storing hazardous items out of reach, securing furniture, using age-appropriate toys and activities, covering electrical outlets, and keeping floors clean and dry. Additionally, emergency preparedness measures such as having a first-aid kit, knowing CPR, and having emergency contact information readily available can make all the difference in ensuring your grandchildren's safety.

# CHAPTER 5 - NURTURING YOUR GRANDCHILDREN'S GROWTH AND DEVELOPMENT

Being a grandparent is a privilege, and it comes with great responsibility. As a grandparent, you play an essential role in your grandchildren's growth and development. It's your duty to provide them with guidance, love, and support as they navigate their way through life. In this chapter, we will discuss how you can nurture your grandchildren's growth and development by encouraging positive behaviours, developing healthy habits, and promoting learning opportunities.

**Encouraging Positive Behaviours**

Children learn from their surroundings, which means that the environment they grow up in plays a significant role in shaping their behaviour. As a grandparent, it's important to encourage positive behaviours in your grandchildren by creating a positive environment. You can do this by:

- ❖ Praising Good Behaviour – When your grandchildren display good behaviour or make good choices, be sure to praise them wholeheartedly. This builds their confidence and reinforces the idea that good behaviour is valued.

❖ Leading By Example – Your actions speak louder than words. If you want your grandchildren to exhibit positive behaviours such as kindness and respectfulness, model these values in your own behaviour.

❖ Providing Clear Expectations – Be clear about what kind of behaviour is acceptable and what isn't. Provide clear expectations so that there are no uncertainties or confusion.

❖ Encouraging Problem-Solving – Encourage your grandchildren to think critically and solve problems on their own instead of simply telling them what to do.

❖ Listening To Them – Listen actively when your grandchildren talk to you about their feelings or concerns without interrupting them or judging them prematurely.

## Developing Healthy Habits

One of the most valuable things you can do for your grandchildren's growth and development is helping them develop healthy habits early on in life. Habits like healthy eating routines, regular exercise routines, proper sleeping schedules help improve self-esteem while building strong bodies and minds. Here are some things you can do to encourage healthy habits:

❖ Teaching Good Eating Habits – Encourage your grandchildren to eat a well-balanced diet and limit their intake of sweets, fast foods and junk. Make healthy eating tasty, fun and easy to incorporate into their lifestyle.

- ❖ Staying Active – Engage with your grandchildren in activities that stimulate physical activity such as walks, cycling or outdoor games like catch or hide-n-seek. Limit screen time and indoor activities.

- ❖ Promoting Healthy Sleep Habits – Ensure your grandchildren develop good sleep habits by setting up regular bedtimes and ensuring they get enough hours of sleep each night.

- ❖ Educating Them About Health & Safety - Teach them how to stay safe while making smart health choices by providing them with age-appropriate information.

## Promoting Learning Opportunities

Grandparents can play an active role in promoting education among their grandchildren by providing them with learning opportunities outside the classroom. Here are some ways you can promote learning opportunities:

- ❖ Reading Together – Reading is a valuable habit that you can start developing early on in childhood, reading together helps foster reading comprehension, imagination, and critical thinking.

- ❖ Discovering New Interests- Encourage your grandchildren to discover new interests by introducing them to new activities or hobbies they might be interested in exploring, this broadens their horizons intellectually.

- ❖ Encouraging Creativity - Let your grandkids explore their creative side through art projects or music lessons which help develop self-expression, creativity, fine motor skills and emotional intelligence.

- ❖ Facilitating Hands-On Experiences- Provide educational

experiences such as visits to museums, science centres or other interesting places that align with their interests and curiosities.

As grandparents, it's our responsibility to provide our grandchildren with love, guidance, and support as they grow up into successful adults who make positive contributions towards society. By nurturing our children's growth and development through positive behaviours, healthy habits and learning opportunities we can create a positive impact that lasts a lifetime. Start today by incorporating these little steps into your daily interactions with your grandchildren and watch the transformation unfold.

# CHAPTER 6 - ENCOURAGING CREATIVITY THROUGH PLAYTIME

In this chapter, we will discuss ways to encourage creativity through playtime with your grandchildren. It is important for children to express their creativity and imagination, and as a loving grandparent, you can play an important role in fostering these skills.

One way to encourage creativity is through games that promote imaginative thinking. Games like "Story Cubes" or "Imaginiff" are perfect for engaging kids' imaginations. Story Cubes are a set of dice with different pictures on each side. Players roll the dice and then have to create a story based on the images they see. This game allows children to exercise their storytelling abilities and use their imagination to create unique narratives.

Imaginiff is another great game that promotes creativity. In this game, players take turns being the subject of a question, such as "imaginiff you were an animal, what would you be?" Other players then have to guess what the subject's answer would be. This game encourages kids to think outside of the box and come up with creative answers.

Another way to encourage creativity is through DIY craft projects. Craft projects can range from simple activities such as colouring books or painting sets, all the way up to more complex projects like building a birdhouse or making jewellery. These types of activities allow children to express themselves creatively while also developing their fine motor skills.

When choosing craft projects, keep in mind your grandchildren's ages and skill levels. Younger children may enjoy simple activities such as finger painting or drawing with crayons, while older kids may prefer more complicated projects like pottery or sewing.

Encouraging stories and imaginative play is yet another way you can foster creativity in your grandchildren. Storytelling is an excellent activity that stimulates a child's imagination and helps them develop language skills while also encouraging them to think creatively.

You can tell stories orally from memory or read books with your grandchildren, taking turns reading aloud. You can also encourage imaginative play by providing dress-up clothes, puppets or other toys that allow children to act out their own stories and create their own worlds.

Encourage your grandchildren to think of themselves as characters in a story and ask them to imagine what they would do in different situations. This type of activity inspires creativity and allows children to explore new ideas and perspectives.

In conclusion, there are many ways you can encourage creativity through playtime with your grandchildren. Games that promote imaginative thinking, DIY craft projects, and storytelling all provide opportunities for children to express themselves creatively while having fun at the same time. As a loving grandparent, it is important that you embrace these activities and take the time to foster your grandchildren's imagination and creativity.

# CHAPTER 7 - SUPPORTING YOUR GRANDCHILDREN'S EMOTIONAL WELL-BEING

Being a grandparent is not just about spoiling your grandchildren with treats and gifts. It's also about being there for them during tough times, providing a listening ear, and helping them manage their emotions. In this chapter, we will discuss some practical tips on how you can support your grandchildren's emotional well-being.

### Identifying Emotions in Children

The first step in supporting your grandchildren's emotional well-being is identifying their emotions. Children often experience a wide range of emotions, including happiness, sadness, anger, fear, and frustration. However, they may not always have the language to express how they feel.

As a grandparent, you can help by paying attention to their nonverbal cues such as facial expressions and body language. For example, if your grandchild is frowning or crying, they may be feeling sad or upset. If they are stomping their feet or clenching their fists, they may be feeling angry.

Another way to identify your grandchildren's emotions is by asking open-ended questions that encourage them to express themselves. For instance, "What made you feel happy today?" or "How did that make you feel?" These questions can help your grandchild identify and label their emotions.

## Helping Kids Manage Their Emotions

Once you have identified your grandchildren's emotions, the next step is helping them manage these feelings effectively. One way to do this is by teaching them coping mechanisms such as deep breathing exercises or taking a break from the situation when feeling overwhelmed.

It's also important to provide reassurance during challenging situations. As a grandparent, you have a wealth of life experience that you can draw from to offer guidance and encouragement when needed.

For example, if your grandchild has had an argument with a friend at school and feels upset about it, you could say something like "It's okay to feel angry right now; it's natural. But remember that tomorrow is a new day and things will get better." This type of support can help your grandchild feel more optimistic about their situation and less alone in their emotions.

## Building Self-esteem and Confidence

Finally, building self-esteem and confidence is another important aspect of supporting your grandchildren's emotional well-being. Children who have high self-esteem are better equipped to handle difficult situations, make good decisions, and develop healthy relationships with others.

One way to build self-esteem is by praising your grandchildren for their efforts rather than just their achievements. For example, if your grandchild works hard on a school project but doesn't receive the highest grade, you could say "I'm proud of you for trying your best on this project. It shows that you are committed to learning."

Another way to boost your grandchild's confidence is by providing opportunities for them to try new things and take risks. Encouraging them to step outside of their comfort zone can help them develop resilience and overcome challenges.

**Conclusion**

Being a grandparent means being there for your grandchildren in all aspects of their lives, including when it comes to managing their emotions. Identifying emotions, helping kids manage these feelings effectively, and building self-esteem and confidence are all ways that you can support your grandchildren's emotional well-being.

Remember that children need positive role models in their lives who can guide them through life's ups and downs. By providing unconditional love, support, and encouragement as a grandparent, you can help foster a sense of emotional security in your grandchildren that will stay with them throughout their lives.

# CHAPTER 8 - MAKING MEMORIES WITH YOUR FAMILY

**Creating Family Traditions**

As a grandma, one of the most important things you can do is to create family traditions that your grandchildren will remember for years to come. Whether it's an annual holiday celebration or a weekly Sunday dinner, these traditions will help build strong family bonds and provide a sense of belonging.

To start creating traditions, think about what was important in your own life growing up. Did your family have any special holiday traditions? How did you celebrate birthdays or other milestones? You can use these as a starting point for creating new traditions with your own family.

**Some ideas for family traditions include:**

- Cooking a special meal together on holidays
- Going on an annual camping trip
- Having a game night every Friday
- Taking an annual family photo
- Decorating the house for each season

The possibilities are endless! The key is to find activities that everyone enjoys and make them part of your regular routine.

**Celebrating Milestones Together**

As your grandchildren grow up, there will be many milestones to celebrate. From first steps and first words to graduations and weddings, these moments are important not only for the person experiencing them but for the whole family.

When celebrating milestones with your family, it's important to make sure everyone feels included. This may mean adjusting plans based on individual needs or preferences. For example, if one grandchild has food allergies, be sure to choose a restaurant or menu that accommodates their needs.

**Other ideas for celebrating milestones include:**

- ❖ Hosting a party or dinner at home
- ❖ Taking a special trip together
- ❖ Creating a scrapbook or photo album of memories

Remember that the most important thing is to show your love and support during these milestone moments. Take lots of photos and enjoy being together as a family.

**Planning Activities for Special Occasions**

Whether it's Christmas, Easter or Halloween, there are always special occasions throughout the year that provide opportunities for fun family activities. As a grandma, you can help plan and organize these activities to make them even more memorable.

**Some ideas for special occasion activities include:**

- ❖ Decorate the house together for the holiday
- ❖ Bake cookies or other treats
- ❖ Have a themed dinner or party
- ❖ Go on a hayride or pumpkin patch adventure

When planning activities, it's important to keep everyone's interests and abilities in mind. For example, younger grandchildren may not be able to participate in more physically demanding activities, while older grandchildren may not enjoy crafts or games meant for younger children.

## Final Thoughts

As a grandma, you have a unique opportunity to create lasting memories with your family. Whether it's through traditions, milestone celebrations or special occasion activities, your love and creativity can help bring your family closer together.

Remember that the most important thing is to enjoy being together as a family. Laugh, have fun, and cherish every moment you spend with your grandchildren. These memories will last a lifetime and will be cherished by generations to come.

# CHAPTER 9 - FINANCIAL PLANNING FOR YOUR GRANDCHILDREN

As a grandparent, you want to be able to provide the best for your grandchildren in every way possible. One of the most important aspects that require careful consideration is financial planning.

In this chapter, we'll discuss various ways in which you can help your grandchildren financially. Whether it's setting up a college fund or looking into available financial aid options, we've got you covered.

**Setting up a College Fund**

College education is becoming increasingly expensive with each passing year. As a grandparent, you can make an enormous impact on the lives of your grandchildren by helping them pay for their college education.

One of the most effective ways to do this is by setting up a college fund. A 529 savings plan is an excellent option for grandparents who want to save money for their grandkids' college education. This plan offers tax-deferred growth and tax-free withdrawals when used towards eligible educational expenses.

There are two types of 529 plans - prepaid tuition plans and education savings plans. A prepaid tuition plan allows grandparents to pay for future college expenses at today's rates, while an education savings plan lets them invest money that grows tax-free until it's withdrawn.

It's important to note that contributions made towards a 529 plan are considered gifts and are subject to gift-tax rules. Currently, grandparents can contribute up to $15,000 annually without having to pay any gift tax.

## Saving Tips for Families with Younger Kids

If your grandchildren are still very young, you might be wondering how you can help them financially before they're even thinking about college. The good news is that there are plenty of saving tips that families with younger kids can take advantage of.

Firstly, consider opening a custodial account for your grandchild. This type of account allows you to transfer ownership of assets like stocks, bonds, or mutual funds directly to your grandchild once they reach legal age. It can be a great way to start building their financial portfolio early on in life.

Another option is to contribute to a 529 plan as mentioned earlier. If the parents have already opened one, you can make contributions towards it as well.

Encouraging your grandchildren to save money themselves is also an excellent way to teach them the value of money. You could set up a savings account for them and encourage them to save any money they receive from birthdays, holidays, or other occasions.

## Available Financial Aid Options

Despite your best efforts, sometimes there may still be a gap between what you've saved and what your grandchild needs for college expenses. In such cases, it's essential to explore available financial aid options.

One of the most common forms of financial aid is federal student loans. These loans are typically offered at lower interest rates than private loans and may be subsidized by the government.

Another option is scholarships. Many colleges and universities offer scholarships based on academic achievements, athletic abilities, or other criteria. Encourage your grandchild to apply for as many scholarships as possible - every little bit helps!

Finally, work-study programs can also provide valuable assistance. These programs allow students to earn money while attending school by working part-time jobs on campus.

## Conclusion

Financial planning for your grandchildren requires careful consideration and planning. Whether it's setting up a college fund or exploring available financial aid options, there are several ways that you can help your grandchild achieve their educational goals without breaking the bank.

Remember that the earlier you start saving, the better off you'll be in the long run. By taking advantage of different saving tips and exploring various financial aid options, you'll be able to make an enormous impact on your grandchild's future success.

# CHAPTER 10 - PASSING ON CULTURAL HERITAGE TO FUTURE GENERATIONS

One of the greatest gifts a grandparent can give to their grandchildren is passing on their cultural heritage. It's important for children to know where they come from, to understand their family history, and embrace their cultural roots. This chapter will cover some tips and ideas for grandparents who want to pass on their cultural heritage to future generations.

## Learning About Your Family History

The first step in passing on cultural heritage is learning about your family history. Spend time with older relatives and ask them about their lives growing up, how they celebrated holidays or special events, what traditions they had, and what challenges they faced. Record these stories in a journal or even better, video record them so that your grandchildren can hear directly from their ancestors.

Another great way to learn about your family history is through genealogy research. There are many resources available online such as ancestry websites and historical archives that can help you trace your family's lineage back several generations. You can share this information with your grandchildren and show them how far back their roots go.

## Teaching Culture Through Food, Music, or Arts

Food is an integral part of any culture and sharing traditional dishes with grandchildren could be a fun bonding experience while passing on cultural heritage at the same time. Teach your grandkids how to cook traditional meals that have been passed down through generations in your family. Explain how certain ingredients are used specifically in certain dishes- for example cumin being used heavily in Indian cuisine. Cooking together will not only keep the traditions alive but it also provides an opportunity for some quality time spent together while enjoying each other's company.

Music is another powerful tool for teaching culture; expose children to music that has special meaning within your own culture or country of origin whether it's traditional folk songs or contemporary pop music by artists who represent that culture well. Share the stories behind the songs so children become invested in learning about both the music and culture. If possible, attend a live concert or event that showcases the music of your culture to give children the full experience.

Arts and crafts are another way for grandparents to pass on cultural heritage. Traditional art forms such as painting, pottery or weaving might be passed down in a family, but you could also teach your grandchildren how to make traditional handicrafts of your own culture like origami or how to make paper mache masks as part of a festival celebration. This is an opportunity for them to not only learn about their heritage but also have an opportunity to develop their creativity.

## Preserving Heirlooms and Artefacts

Another way grandparents can preserve their cultural heritage is by passing on heirlooms and artefacts that have been handed down through generations of the family. Examples of these could include: jewellery, clothing (like saris from India), traditional clothing pieces like kilts from Scotland and even musical instruments. Tell your grandchildren about why these pieces are important and what they symbolize in your culture's history.

If you don't have any heirlooms or artefacts that can be passed on, consider creating new ones special for the family- start with the basics like personalised jewellery gifts or embroidered handkerchiefs. These could be customised with traditional designs unique to your culture so that future generations can look back fondly at special memories spent together with their grandparents.

In conclusion, there are many ways grandparents can pass on their cultural heritage to future generations. Learning about family history, teaching culture through food, music or arts while preserving heirlooms & artefacts is one way, they can do it. The most important thing is to take an active role in imparting knowledge about the values, traditions, and beliefs specific to your roots that create a sense of pride in both the past and present generations- after all this legacy will move forward providing our children with insights into who they are as individuals shaped by their family history.

# CHAPTER 11 - MAINTAINING A HEALTHY LIFESTYLE

When it comes to being the best grandma in the world, it's important to not only create lasting memories with your grandchildren but also to ensure that they are leading healthy lives. As grandparents, we have a responsibility to instil good habits in our grandchildren and one of the most important habits is maintaining a healthy lifestyle.

**Encouraging a Balanced Diet**

As grandparents, we often find ourselves indulging our grandchildren with sweet treats and delicious snacks. While it's okay to indulge once in a while, it's important to encourage a balanced diet. Make sure that your grandchildren are eating plenty of fruits, vegetables, whole grains, and lean protein.

One way you can promote healthy eating is by involving your grandchildren in meal planning and preparation. Take them grocery shopping and let them pick out their favourite fruits and vegetables. Teach them how to prepare simple meals like salads, sandwiches, or scrambled eggs.

Another great idea is to involve your grandchildren in cooking lessons. This will help them develop an appreciation for healthy foods and inspire them to try new things. Plus, cooking together can be fun and provide quality bonding time.

**Exercise Routines for Kids and Adults**

Physical activity is essential for maintaining a healthy lifestyle. As grandparents, we should encourage regular exercise activities for our grandchildren as well as ourselves.

For kids, there are plenty of fun exercises that can get them moving such as dancing, playing sports or going on bike rides. You could also take them on nature walks or hikes which will not only provide physical activity but also give you both quality time together in nature.

Moreover, adults too need routine exercise activities for staying fit and active- so why not incorporate some fun exercises into your daily routine? Try taking yoga classes together or going on morning walks around the neighbourhood. It doesn't matter what activities you choose as long as they're enjoyable enough that you'll stick with it.

**Making Health a Priority**

It's important to make health a priority in our lives, not just for ourselves but also for our grandchildren. We can lead by example and show them how to live an active and healthy lifestyle. Here are some tips on how to make health a priority:

**1. Plan regular check-ups with your doctor**

Make sure you and your grandchildren are up to date with all necessary check-ups, such as dental appointments, eye exams, and physicals. A proactive approach will help prevent illnesses before they become serious.

**2. Get enough sleep**

Getting enough sleep is essential for good health, both mentally and physically. Encourage your grandchildren to establish a bedtime routine that provides ample time for restful sleep.

**3. Reduce screen time**

Excess screen time can negatively affect children's development and well-being. Limit the amount of time your grandchildren spend in front of screens, whether it's TV, video games or smartphones.

**4. Practise mindfulness**

Mindfulness practices like meditation or deep breathing can help reduce stress levels which can have significant positive impacts on both children and adults alike.

In conclusion, maintaining a healthy lifestyle is crucial in leading happy and fulfilling lives as grandparents/grandchildren or individuals. By promoting balanced diets, regular exercise routines, and making health a priority in our daily lives- we can set a great example for our grandchildren while also enjoying the benefits of better physical fitness and overall well-being ourselves!

# CHAPTER 12 - THE IMPORTANCE OF GRANDPARENTING IN SINGLE-PARENT HOUSEHOLDS

Being a grandparent is one of life's greatest joys. Many grandparents relish the opportunity to spoil their grandchildren, but being a grandparent is about so much more than just giving out presents and treats. It's about providing support and love for your family, especially when times are tough. Being a grandparent can be especially important in single-parent households, where the challenges can be greater for both the parent and child.

## Understanding the Challenges Faced by Single Parents

Single parenthood can be a challenging experience, no matter what age or stage of life you're in. Whether you're a young single mother struggling to make ends meet or an older single father who has recently lost a spouse, being a single parent requires patience, dedication, and strength.

One of the biggest challenges that single parents face is lack of support. Without a partner to rely on, single parents often find themselves juggling work, home responsibilities and childcare all on their own. This can lead to exhaustion and burnout, which can negatively impact both the parent and child.

Another challenge for single parents is financial strain. Raising children on one income is never easy, and many single parents struggle to provide basic necessities such as food, clothing, and shelter for their children. This is where grandparents can step in to offer support.

**Ways to Support Single Parents**

There are many ways that grandparents can support single parents in their family unit:

- ❖ Offer emotional support - One of the most important things that grandparents can do for their grandchildren and their adult children is offer emotional support during difficult times. Let them know that they are loved unconditionally and that you will always be there for them when they need someone to talk to.

- ❖ Provide practical help - Grandparents can also provide practical help such as babysitting or picking up groceries for the family. Even small gestures like taking your grandchild to the park or making them dinner can make a huge difference in the life of a single parent.

- ❖ Financial assistance - If you are able, offering financial assistance to your adult child can help ease the burden of single parenthood. Whether it's paying for school supplies or helping with rent, every little bit helps.

- ❖ Be available - Being available is crucial when it comes to supporting single parents. Make sure that your adult child knows that they can call you any time of day or night if they need help or just someone to talk to.

**Providing Consistent Support to Your Grandchildren**

Consistency is key when it comes to being a supportive grandparent in a single-parent household. It's important to be there for your grandchildren on a regular basis, whether it's once a week for dinner or every other weekend for an overnight visit.

**Grandparents can provide consistency in many ways:**

- ❖ Provide stability - Single parents often struggle to provide stability for their children due to work obligations and other responsibilities. By providing consistent routines and traditions, such as weekly dinners or annual family vacations, grandparents can help provide stability and security for their grandchildren.

- ❖ Offer guidance - Grandparents have years of experience raising children and can offer valuable guidance and advice for their adult children who are navigating parenthood on their own.

- ❖ Foster relationships - Grandparents also play an important role in fostering relationships between siblings and extended family members. By hosting family gatherings and encouraging regular communication, grandparents can help keep family bonds strong even in difficult times.

In conclusion, being a grandparent is all about love and support, especially in single-parent households where the challenges can be even greater than usual. By understanding the challenges faced by single parents, providing emotional support and practical help, offering financial assistance if possible, being available at all times, providing stability and guidance consistently; grandparents can make a huge difference in the lives of both their adult children and grandchildren. Remember, the relationship between grandparents and grandchildren is a special one that can never be replaced, so cherish it always.

# CHAPTER 13 - ACCEPTING CHANGES AS YOUR GRANDCHILDREN GROW

As a grandmother, you have probably witnessed some of the most momentous changes in your grandchildren's lives. From their first steps and words to their first day at school, everything is a milestone that fills us with pride and joy.

But as they grow older, your role as a grandparent will also change. It can be challenging to accept these changes and adapt to them, but it's important if you want to stay relevant in their lives and maintain a strong bond.

In this chapter, we'll cover three aspects of accepting changes as your grandchildren grow: coping with different stages of life, embracing technological advancements and trends, and being a positive influence while allowing independence.

**Coping with Different Stages of Life**

One of the biggest challenges in accepting changes as your grandchildren grow is coping with different stages of life.

Whether your grandkids are toddlers or teenagers, each age presents its unique joys and struggles.

For example, when your grandchild is a toddler, you may spend hours playing with building blocks or reading picture books. But when they become teenagers, they may not be interested in these activities anymore. Instead, they might want to spend more time on their phones or hanging out with friends.

It's essential to remember that these changes don't mean that your grandkids love you any less. They're just growing up and exploring new things. Here are some tips for coping with these different stages:

- ❖ Be flexible: As your grandchild grows older, their hobbies and interests will likely change too. Being flexible means being open-minded about spending time together doing things that interest them or trying something new together.
- ❖ Stay involved: Even if your grandchild seems less interested in spending time with you, it's important to stay involved in their life. Ask them about their interests and activities regularly and show interest in what they're doing.
- ❖ Don't take it personally: Sometimes, your grandkids might say hurtful things or seem distant. It's important to remember that it's not about you – it's a part of growing up and finding their own identity.

## Embracing Technological Advancements and Trends

The world is changing rapidly, and technology has become an essential part of our daily lives. While some grandparents might feel intimidated by these changes, it's essential to embrace them if you want to maintain a strong relationship with your grandkids.

**Here are some tips for embracing technology:**

❖ Learn from your grandchildren: Your grandkids are likely more tech-savvy than you are, so don't be afraid to ask them for help or advice. They'll probably love the opportunity to teach you something new!

❖ Keep up to date: Technology is constantly evolving, so make sure you keep up to date with the latest trends and advancements. This can help you better understand what your grandkids are interested in and make conversations more engaging.

❖ Set boundaries: While technology can be a great tool for staying connected with your grandkids, it's important to set boundaries around how much time you spend on devices. Too much screen time can have negative effects on mental health and relationships.

## Being a Positive Influence While Allowing Independence

As your grandchildren grow older, they'll start to become more independent and make their own decisions. While this can be tough to accept sometimes, it's crucial to allow them the freedom they need while still being a positive influence in their life.

**Here are some tips:**

- ❖ Be supportive: Even if you don't always agree with your grandchild's choices, it's essential to remain supportive of them. Show interest in their goals and dreams and encourage them along the way.

- ❖ Share wisdom: As someone with more life experience than your grandchild, you have valuable knowledge and wisdom to share. But instead of forcing advice on them, try to offer guidance gently and only when asked.

- ❖ Respect their boundaries: As your grandchild grows older, they'll likely have more boundaries around what they're comfortable sharing with you. It's important to respect these boundaries and avoid prying or asking too many personal questions.

## Conclusion

Accepting changes as your grandchildren grow can be challenging, but it's essential if you want to maintain a strong and meaningful relationship with them. By coping with different stages of life, embracing technological advancements and trends, and being a positive influence while allowing independence, you can stay relevant in their lives and continue to make memories together.

# CHAPTER 14 - BEING AN ADVOCATE FOR YOUR GRANDCHILDREN'S EDUCATION

Being a grandparent is one of the most rewarding experiences in life. You get to watch your children grow up and start families of their own, while also having the opportunity to impact the lives of your grandchildren. One of the best ways you can do that is by being an advocate for their education.

**Supporting Education Goals**

As grandparents, it's important to be supportive of your grandchildren's education goals. Whether they're striving to get straight A's, pursuing a specific career path, or simply trying to pass their classes, make sure they know that you're there for them every step of the way.

Encourage them to set realistic goals and work hard towards achieving them. Celebrate their successes with them and offer guidance when they face challenges. Let them know that no matter what happens, you believe in them and are proud of their efforts.

## Navigating School Policies and Systems

In today's educational landscape, schools have many policies and systems in place that can sometimes be difficult to navigate. As a grandparent, it's important to familiarize yourself with these policies so that you can better support your grandchild's education.

For example, learn about the school's attendance policy so that you can help ensure your grandchild doesn't miss too much class time. Find out how grades are weighted and calculated so that you can offer study tips or connect them with tutors if needed.

Additionally, learn about any extracurricular activities or clubs offered at the school so that you can encourage your grandchild to explore different interests.

If your grandchild has any special needs or learning challenges, it may be beneficial to attend parent-teacher conferences or meetings with school administrators to discuss accommodations on behalf of your grandchild. Be sure to also inform yourself about any resources available through the school district such as special education programs or counselling services.

**Engaging in Your Grandchild's Learning Journey**

One of the most impactful ways to be an advocate for your grandchildren's education is by actively engaging in their learning journey. One of the best things you can do is simply be present and show interest in what they're learning.

For example, ask about their favourite subjects and why they enjoy them. Ask about upcoming projects or assignments and offer to help if they need it. Attend school functions such as parent-teacher conferences or back-to-school nights so that you can meet their teachers and see first-hand what they're learning.

Additionally, consider sharing your own interests or hobbies with them. If you love science, take them on a nature walk and point out interesting flora and fauna. If you enjoy cooking, teach them how to make a family recipe. Not only will these experiences create lasting memories, but they'll also help your grandchild learn new skills and expand their knowledge base.

Supporting your grandchild's education doesn't have to be overly complicated or time-consuming. Simply showing up and being present goes a long way in letting them know that you care about their success both inside and outside of the classroom.

In conclusion, being an advocate for your grandchildren's

education means supporting their goals, navigating school policies and systems, and engaging in their learning journey. By doing so, you can help ensure that they have the tools and resources needed to succeed academically while also fostering a lifelong love of learning. Remember, each day is a chance to make a positive impact on your grandchild's life. Seize it!

# CHAPTER 15 - ENCOURAGING SOCIALIZATION SKILLS IN YOUR GRANDKIDS

Being a grandparent is not just about spoiling your grandkids with treats and gifts. It's also about providing guidance and support to help them become well-adjusted and socially adept individuals. In this chapter, we'll explore ways to encourage socialization skills in your grandkids.

**Building Connections with Peers**

One of the most important aspects of socialization is building connections with peers. As a grandparent, you can help facilitate these connections by encouraging your grandkids to participate in activities that involve other children. This can include organized sports teams, art classes, or even playdates with friends.

It's important to remember that socializing doesn't come naturally to everyone, especially children who are shy or introverted. If you notice that your grandkid is having difficulty making friends, don't force them into situations that make them uncomfortable. Instead, try to find activities that match their interests and provide opportunities for them to meet like-minded kids.

## Developing Social Skills Through Playtime

Playtime provides an excellent opportunity for kids to develop their social skills without feeling pressured or overwhelmed. Whether it's playing board games, building forts, or having tea parties, playing with others helps kids learn how to share, take turns, and resolve conflicts.

As a grandparent, you can help facilitate positive play experiences for your grandkids by setting up an area in your home where they can play freely and comfortably. Make sure there are plenty of toys and games available that encourage interaction between players. You can also plan special activities like baking cookies together or going on a nature walk.

It's important to let kids take charge of their playtime while still providing guidance when needed. Encourage them to work together on projects and discuss how they can best tackle challenges as a team.

## Promoting Teamwork and Collaboration

Teamwork and collaboration are essential social skills that will serve your grandkids well into adulthood. Whether it's working on a school project or participating in a sports team, learning how to work with others towards a common goal is an important life skill.

As a grandparent, you can promote teamwork and collaboration by encouraging your grandkids to participate in group activities. This can include things like volunteering together or organizing a family game night where everyone works together towards a common goal.

It's also important to model positive behaviours when it comes to teamwork and collaboration. If your grandkids see you working well with others, they are more likely to follow suit. Encourage open communication, active listening, and compromise when working with others.

**Final Thoughts**

Encouraging socialization skills in your grandkids is an important part of being the best grandma in the world. By building connections with peers, facilitating positive play experiences, and promoting teamwork and collaboration, you'll be helping your grandkids develop essential social skills that will serve them well throughout their lives.

Remember to provide guidance and support while still allowing your grandkids to take charge of their own social experiences. With your help and encouragement, they'll be well on their way to becoming socially competent individuals who are equipped to handle any situation that comes their way.

# CHAPTER 16 - MANAGING BEHAVIOURAL ISSUES EFFECTIVELY

As a grandmother, dealing with your grandchild's behavioural issues can be tricky. You want to be the fun and loving grandma, but you also need to maintain some level of discipline and boundaries. In this chapter, we'll discuss how to manage behavioural issues effectively, including dealing with tantrums, whining, or other outbursts. We'll also explore discipline methods that work without harshness while maintaining boundaries and rules.

**Dealing with Tantrums, Whining, or Other Outbursts**

As much as we love our grandchildren, there are moments when they can become quite difficult to handle. Dealing with tantrums, whining, or other outbursts can be frustrating for both you and your grandchild. The key is to stay calm and patient while addressing the issue.

Firstly, try to identify the reason behind their tantrum or outburst. Are they hungry or tired? Did something specific trigger their behaviour? Once you have identified the cause of their outburst, address it appropriately. If they are hungry or tired, offer them a snack or suggest taking a nap.

Secondly, validate their emotions by acknowledging how they feel. For example, if your grandchild is upset because they cannot have ice cream before dinner, tell them "I know you really want ice cream right now and it is hard not getting what we want sometimes". This helps them understand that their emotions are important and heard.

Thirdly establish clear boundaries about what behaviour is acceptable when expressing those feelings. While validating emotions make sure your child understands the boundary - "It's okay to feel angry but throwing things around isn't okay."

## Discipline Methods that Work Without Harshness

Disciplining your grandchild doesn't always mean resorting to harsh punishment methods like spanking or yelling. Instead of using fear as a motivator for good behaviour, use positive reinforcement techniques such as praising good behaviour often. Instead of punishing bad behaviour, focus on redirecting them towards other activities or behaviours.

If your grandchild is misbehaving, set clear boundaries and expectations so they understand what is expected of them. Explain the consequences of not following these boundaries in a calm and firm way. Make sure to praise them when they follow the rules and meet expectations.

## Maintaining Boundaries and Rules

As grandparents, we may feel guilty for setting boundaries or rules with our grandkids. However, healthy boundaries are essential for their safety, well-being, and development. It's important to remember that children crave structure, consistency, and predictability especially in situations where parents are absent or busy.

Consistency is key when it comes to enforcing rules. That means both parents adhere to the same guidelines around things like screen time or appropriate language use. This reduces chances of confusion among children.

Lastly, make sure your grandchild understands why certain rules have been put in place. Explain it to them calmly without sounding harsh - "We don't run in the house because someone could slip and fall".

In conclusion, managing behavioural issues effectively as a grandma requires patience, understanding and consistent discipline techniques. By staying calm while addressing tantrums, validating their emotions while setting clear boundaries regarding behaviour, using positive reinforcement techniques instead of harsh punishment methods, and enforces consistent rules you can create a healthy balance between being a fun-loving grandma while still maintaining some level of structure in your grandchild's life. Remember though that even with everything said above, children will be children but by being there for them consistently through good days and bad you too can be the "best grandma" in their eyes!

# CHAPTER 17 - BONDING WITH TEENAGE GRANDCHILDREN

As our grandchildren grow and develop, their personalities and interests change. When they reach their teenage years, it can be challenging to maintain a close relationship with them. However, there are ways to connect with your teenage grandchildren and build a meaningful bond.

**Understanding Teenage Behaviour**

Teenagers experience a wide range of emotions as they navigate through this stage of life. They may feel self-conscious, anxious, or rebellious as they try to find their place in the world. As grandparents, we can be supportive and understanding by listening actively without passing judgement. We should also respect their need for privacy and independence.

## Connecting Despite Generational Differences

A generation gap can exist between grandparents and teenagers due to differences in upbringing, culture, and exposure to technology. To bridge this gap, grandparents should take an interest in what's important to their teenage grandchildren. This could include music, fashion, social media, or sports. Engaging in activities that the teenager enjoys is a great way to show support for them.

It's essential not only to listen but also be open minded about things that might not appeal to us at first glance. Instead of approaching these situations with judgement or criticism, consider asking questions about how this new thing works or why it's exciting for her/him.

## Building Trust and Respect

To connect effectively with our teenage grandchildren, we must aim for mutual trust and respect. Here are some ways we can achieve that:

- ❖ Communicate openly - Let the teenager know they can confide in you if they need someone to talk to.
- ❖ Be reliable - Stick to commitments made regarding time spent together.
- ❖ Show interest in their lives - Ask about their interests, achievements, and goals.
- ❖ Don't push boundaries - Respect boundaries set by teenagers while still being available when needed.
- ❖ Understand differing perspectives - Accept that teenagers may have different opinions on things than you do.

## Conclusion

Bonding with teenage grandchildren is all about understanding, communicating, and building trust. Teenagers need our support, encouragement, and guidance as they navigate this challenging stage of life. By showing respect and interest in their lives, we can develop a meaningful relationship that will last a lifetime.

# CHAPTER 18 - APPROACHING SENSITIVE TOPICS WITH YOUR GRANDCHILDREN

As a grandparent, you want to protect your grandchildren from the harsh realities of life. However, at times, there are situations that demand talking about sensitive topics such as death, divorce, bullying, and so on. It can be challenging to approach such subjects without overwhelming or scaring them. In this chapter, we will discuss how to initiate these conversations and create a safe space for communication.

## Addressing Sensitive Topics Such as Death, Divorce, Bullying, Etc.

Death is an inevitable part of life; it is natural to feel overwhelmed when discussing it with children. Be honest but gentle when explaining death to your grandchildren. Begin by asking what they understand about the subject and clear any misconceptions they might have. Use age-appropriate language; younger children may have difficulty grasping the full concept of death.

Divorce is another difficult topic that can affect your grandchildren's emotions. As grandparents, you need to ensure that you do not take sides and remain unbiased while having discussions around separation or divorce in the family. Try not to speak ill of either party involved and maintain neutrality no matter what.

Bullying is a prevalent issue in today's society that needs addressing delicately. Children may feel scared or ashamed when being bullied; hence creating a safe space for them to share their experiences becomes paramount. Encourage your grandchildren to communicate openly with you by listening actively without interrupting or judging them.

## Creating Safe Spaces for Communication

Creating an environment where your grandkids can communicate freely about sensitive topics is crucial in helping them feel supported and understood. Ensure that your grandkids know they can come to you at any time if they need someone to talk to or share their feelings with.

Normalizing open communication will encourage children not only to talk about issues concerning them but also create awareness around respecting different opinions and learning how differences in perspectives can lead us to appreciate and understand each other better. Using positive language and acknowledging the emotion behind their words can help to build trust and foster a deeper relationship with them.

## Helping Them Cope with Emotional Turmoil

Learning how to deal with emotional turmoil is essential for children's mental health, enabling them to develop resilience in challenging situations. It's important to teach your grandchildren healthy coping mechanisms such as taking a break, deep breathing exercises or practicing mindfulness.

Encourage your grandkids that expressing emotions such as

anger, sadness or frustration is healthy, but helping them channel these emotions towards forming constructive solutions will make a tremendous difference in their lives. As grandparents, you can also teach them problem-solving skills by encouraging them to brainstorm solutions together.

In conclusion, talking about sensitive topics with your grandchildren may not be easy; however, it's crucial in helping them navigate through life's challenges. Normalizing discussions around death, divorce and bullying while creating safe spaces for communication can go a long way in building stronger bonds with your grandkids. Furthermore, teaching them healthy ways of coping with emotional turmoil prepares them to lead healthier lives ahead.

# CHAPTER 19 - SURVIVING LONG-DISTANCE RELATIONSHIPS WITH YOUR GRANDKIDS

As much as we would love to spend every moment with our grandchildren, sometimes distance gets in the way. Whether they live across the country or across the world, long-distance relationships can be challenging. However, with some effort and creativity, you can still maintain a strong bond with your grandkids.

**Keeping Communication Lines Open**

Communication is key in any relationship, and this rings especially true in long-distance grandparenting. Thanks to modern technology, there are now more ways than ever to stay connected with your grandkids. Here are some tips for keeping those communication lines open:

- ❖ Video calls - Apps like Skype, FaceTime and Zoom allow you to talk face-to-face with your grandkids even if you're miles apart. Set aside regular times for video calls so that you can catch up on each other's lives.

❖ Texting - Sometimes a quick message is all it takes to let your grandkids know that you're thinking of them. Use apps like WhatsApp or iMessage to stay in touch throughout the day.

❖ Social media - If your grandkids are old enough to use social media platforms like Facebook or Instagram, follow them and comment on their posts. This will show them that you're interested in their lives even from afar.

**Maximizing Technology to Stay Connected**

Besides traditional forms of communication, you can also take advantage of technology to make long-distance relationships more engaging and interactive:

1. Play games together online - There are plenty of online games that can be played together over video chat or messaging apps. Games like Words With Friends or Draw Something are both fun and easy to play remotely.

2. Watch movies together - Thanks to streaming services like Netflix Party, you can watch movies at the same time as your grandkids even if you're not in the same room.

3. Virtual tours - Many museums and landmarks around the world offer virtual tours that you can experience together with your grandkids. This is a great way to explore the world from the comfort of your own home.

**Planning Visits and Memorializing Moments Together**

While technology can help bridge the distance, nothing beats actual face-to-face time. Here are some tips for making the most of visits with your grandkids:

❖ Plan ahead - Make sure to plan your visits in advance so that everyone has something to look forward to. Talk with your grandkids about what they want to do while you're there and make a loose itinerary.

- ❖ Take lots of pictures and videos - Pictures and videos are a great way to remember special moments spent together. Encourage your grandkids to take pictures too so that you can see things from their perspective.

- ❖ Create a scrapbook or memory book - After each visit, create a scrapbook or memory book together with your grandkids. This will allow them to relive those moments over and over again and strengthen the bond between you.

Long-distance relationships with our grandkids can be tough, but by keeping communication lines open, maximizing technology, and planning meaningful visits, we can still make the most of our time together no matter how far apart we may be.

# CHAPTER 20 - LEAVING A LEGACY AS THE BEST GRANDMA IN THE WORLD

As a grandma, you have the unique opportunity to share your values, wisdom, and experiences with your grandchildren. You can help shape their lives and leave a lasting legacy that will be remembered for generations to come. In this chapter, we'll discuss how to celebrate achievements and accomplishments, build meaningful relationships, and cherish the memories made together.

**Celebrating Achievements and Accomplishments**

One of the best ways to leave a legacy as the best grandma in the world is by celebrating your grandchildren's achievements and accomplishments. Whether it's a big accomplishment like graduating from college or something small like learning how to ride a bike, take time to acknowledge their hard work and efforts.

**You can do this in several ways. For example, you could:**

- ❖ Attend graduations, recitals, or competitions: Showing up to these events will mean so much to your grandchild. It shows that you care about what they're doing and support them every step of the way.

- ❖ Display their artwork or awards: Hang up their artwork or display their trophies or medals in a prominent place in your home. This sends the message that you're proud of them and want everyone else to know about their accomplishments too.

- ❖ Give them a special gift: Consider giving them something meaningful that they can keep forever as a reminder of their achievement. For example, you could give them a piece of jewellery with their birthstone on it or an engraved photo frame.

## Building Meaningful Relationships

Another important aspect of being the best grandma in the world is building meaningful relationships with your grandchildren. This goes beyond just spending time with them - it's about really getting to know them on a deeper level.

**Here are some tips for building meaningful relationships with your grandchildren:**

- ❖ Really listen: When you spend time with your grandkids, make an effort to listen actively to what they're saying. Show genuine interest in their lives and what's important to them.

- ❖ Share your own experiences: Use your own life experiences to connect with your grandchildren. Share stories from your own childhood or talk about a time when you faced a difficult situation and how you overcame it.

- ❖ Be present: When you're spending time with your grandkids, put away the distractions (like your phone) and really be present in the moment. This will show them that they have your full attention and that you value the time you're spending together.

## Cherishing the Memories Made Together

Finally, as the best grandma in the world, it's important to cherish the memories made together. These memories are what will last long after you're gone, so take every opportunity to create special moments with your grandkids.

**Here are some ideas for creating and cherishing memories:**

- ❖ Take photos: Take lots of photos of you and your grandkids doing things together. You can create a scrapbook or photo album that they can keep as a reminder of all the fun times you had.

❖ Start traditions: Establishing traditions is a great way to create lasting memories. For example, maybe every summer you take a trip to the beach together or make cookies together at Christmastime.

❖ Write letters: Consider writing letters to your grandkids that they can open on special occasions (like their birthday or graduation). In these letters, share what you love about them, what makes them special, and why you're proud of them.

In conclusion, being the best grandma in the world is all about leaving a legacy that will be remembered for generations to come. By celebrating achievements and accomplishments, building meaningful relationships, and cherishing the memories made together, you can leave an indelible mark on your grandchildren's lives.

As we come to the end of this book, I hope that you've gained some valuable insights and tips on how to be the best grandma in the world. Remember, being a grandmother is not just about spoiling your grandkids with candy or gifts. It's about providing them with love, guidance, and support as they navigate their way through life.

One thing I always stress is the importance of communication. Take the time to listen to your grandkids and understand their interests, fears, and dreams. Share stories from your own life and experiences, so they can learn from your wisdom.

Don't forget to have fun! Whether it's playing games, going on adventures, or simply spending quality time together, building happy memories will strengthen your bond with your grandkids.

Being a grandma also requires patience and flexibility. Don't get discouraged if things don't go according to plan. Embrace spontaneity and make the most of every moment you have with them.

Lastly, remember that being a grandma is an honour and a privilege. Cherish these moments because before you know it, they'll be all grown up.

If you found yourself enjoying the pages of this book, please help us spread the word by leaving a lovely review and go out there and show everyone how you can be the best grandma in the world!

# ABOUT THE AUTHOR

**A.j. Lowrie**

When not writing, A.J. Lowrie can often be found exploring nature or spending time with family and friends. Drawing inspiration from personal experiences as fuel for writing books.

Printed in Great Britain
by Amazon